For Heaven's Sake: Who Is Jesus?

By
Don Anderson

ISBN: 1-60002-139-5

Unless otherwise noted, Scripture quotations in this book are taken from the HOLY BIBLE, New King James Version, Copyright 1982, Thomas Nelson, Inc.

Table of Contents

1. Who is Jesus?..1

2. Revelation of Jesus 27

3. Further Evidence..57

4. Practical Evidence...77

5. Final Arguments...107

Chapter 1
Who is Jesus?

Many people today believe all religions are essentially the same and worship the same God...that simply is not true.

The messages of numerous religious leaders throughout history proclaim their particular beliefs to their followers. Confucius, Jesus, Buddha, and Mohammed are several of the better-known religious leaders. In the past two hundred years others, such as Joseph Smith and Charles (Taze) Russell, have risen up for a season and then died. Most of these leaders met resistance of some sort, but none to the level that Jesus encountered. Jesus is the name that evokes a myriad of emotions and responses in people of all cultural and religious thinking. No other person has received such microscopic scrutiny. When Jesus was on earth, many devoted their lives to Him, while others wanted to kill Him. Some thought He was a great leader; others said He was a deceiver. Many were persuaded God sent Him to earth, yet others strongly felt that He worked through the power of Satan. So, who is Jesus? This is undoubtedly one of the most debated questions of all time.

Today, ask several people what they think of Jesus, and do not be surprised if no two responses are the same. Even now, Jesus' name still stirs up a wide array of responses. Some give Him the highest respect; others think He is a charlatan. Some people love him with their whole heart; others despise him. Many frequently swear by Him. By doing so, some are taking His name in vain and others are giving Him the highest praise. Over the years, Jesus has been the topic of both written and visual works. Numerous books, starting with the New Testament, contain both positive and negative opinions about Him. Movies portray His life and death, offering a wide spectrum of viewpoints.

Some cast Him in a favorable light; others express critical connotations. Television specials have explored and documented His life. Peter Jennings of ABC moderated a one-hour special program on Jesus' life in June 2000. Jennings interviewed an assortment of religious leaders, gathering information about who they believe Jesus was and why He came to earth. Jesus made several astounding claims that drew a sharp distinction between His own identity and that of others. As a result, although Jesus was a Jew, even among His countrymen there was a wide range of opinions and emotions about Him.

Worldwide there are many religions, and virtually all of them acknowledge Jesus. Only a few organized groups recognize most religious figures; however, most acknowledge that Jesus lived and had great influence. This alone demonstrates the importance of knowing as much about Him as possible. Although many religions recognize His existence, there is wide disagreement concerning who He is. Some claim Jesus was just a good man and a prophet, others say He was a created being of some sort, still others say He was the Son of God. Only one of these positions can be right. If one religious group believes Jesus is a good man and a prophet, they are directly at odds with those believing He is the Son of God, as well as with those believing He is a created being. If Jesus is the Son of God, He cannot be part of creation, for these viewpoints directly oppose each other. Clearly, the fundamental question is: Who is Jesus?

Many people today believe all religions are essentially the same and worship the same God. From the Biblical perspective, that simply is not true. In John 14:6 Jesus said, "I am the way, the truth and the life. No one comes to the Father except through me." The Bible says Jesus is THE WAY, not a way. The Bible teaches He is the way to the Father. A proper understanding of His identity is required for a person to know the Father God. In addition to every major religion acknowledging Jesus, our Julian calendar centers on His birth (A.D., B.C.). Secular merchants and media acknowledge Easter Sunday as the day commemorating Jesus' resurrection. Since Jesus impacts society in so many areas, understanding of His identity becomes a critical focus. For one seeking the truth, the beginning point of research should be gaining as complete an understanding of His identity as possible. This would include gaining all the information available about who He is. There are differing opinions on this, depending on the source of material. This book will focus on what the Bible says about Jesus.

Believing only one religion can be right seems arrogant and offensive to some individuals. In a zealous effort for achieving unity and peace, people often are willing for compromise. Unfortunately, compromising truth leads to error. It is not brash to believe you have the truth. The following sports example illustrates this point. The Tampa Bay Buccaneers won the Super Bowl in 2002. It is not brash for them to say they were the best team in the National Football League for the 2002 season. This fact is in the record books. Knowing the truth about Jesus should bring pride and confidence in that belief. It is not necessary to put people down during a disagreement. Rather, lovingly explain the areas of controversy and let listeners check them out for themselves. One will never win others over by putting down their beliefs. My advice to Christians is to share the Jesus that you know. It is important to explain the distinctions between Christianity and other beliefs, focusing mainly on the claims of Christ.

Jesus is one of the most controversial figures in history. Many people today say He is the Son of God. This statement is Biblically correct. Unfortunately, many religious groups say Jesus is the Son of God, but their meaning is very different from that of evangelical Christianity. When questioning them, it becomes apparent they actually believe He was a created being of some sort. Therefore, in today's spiritual climate, stating Jesus is the Son of God is incomplete. What then, is the best way to portray Jesus and clearly distinguish Christianity's core belief? To agree with the Bible's teachings about Jesus, *Christians must proclaim Him as God in the flesh.*

1 John 2:22-23 reads, "Who is a liar but he who denies that Jesus is the Christ?...Whoever denies the Son does not have the Father either." This verse reinforces the fact that a wrong belief about Jesus' identity ultimately means one does not know the Father either. Denying the Son's deity is also denying the Father. What does the Word of God say about this issue? In John 4:25-26 we find the terms Christ and Messiah are synonymous. Jesus was telling the woman at the well that He was the Messiah. The Old Testament foretold the Messiah's deity. Isaiah 7:14 reads: "the virgin shall conceive and bear a Son and shall call His name Immanuel." In Matthew 1:23 we learn the term Immanuel means God with us.

Someone recently commented that many parents name their sons Immanuel, inferring it is not significant that Jesus was given that term. Human parents naming a son Immanuel is quite different from God stating that Jesus was to be called Immanuel. God told the prophet Isaiah that Jesus was to be given this title. His messenger Isaiah foretold the Messiah's deity many years before His birth. Later on, Isaiah recorded another prophecy about the coming child (Messiah). Isaiah 9:6 states that the child would have many titles. The child's most important title is Mighty God. Think of that! The prophet, under God's direction, clearly enunciated that Jesus would be deity. That was a powerful statement!

The Old Testament contains other passages speaking of the deity of Jesus. Psalm 45:1-9 speaks of the coming King. This psalm is not talking about God the Father, because in verse two we learn that God blessed Him forever. God does not bless Himself. In verses six and seven, we read that the throne of the King is forever. These verses also refer to the King's deity by calling Him God. Hebrews 1:8-9 quotes this passage and advises us that verses six and seven refer to the Son. This validates that the King in Psalm 45 refers to Jesus and His deity.

In Micah 5:2, we find another reference to the coming Messiah. This passage refers to Him as "The One to be Ruler in Israel." Messiah was to come from the tribe of Judah and would be born in Bethlehem. The verse concludes by stating that His "goings forth are from of old, from everlasting." This statement refers to the eternal existence of the coming ruler. Only deity has eternal existence (Genesis 1:1, John 1:1). No created being of any sort can claim eternal existence; only the creator can! Many people believe the Old Testament does not mention Jesus. As already noted, references to Jesus exist in several passages. The prophets wrote that the Messiah (Jesus) was to be deity! Zechariah 12:8-10 provides insight on Jesus. Verse eight says that in the end-times the "Lord" will defend Jerusalem. He will destroy their enemies. Verse 10 gives a vivid description of the Lord. It states that the Jews will "…look on Me whom they pierced." Since the Lord Jesus is the person they pierced, it would indicate that He is deity.

The Old Testament often refers to the deity of Messiah and Jesus, and this teaching prevails throughout the entire Bible. The New Testament contains many passages teaching and referring to Jesus and His divine claims. In John 5:18 the Jews understood that Jesus was claiming equality with the Father, which enraged them to the point of seeking to kill Him. Jesus, the second person of the Trinity, was stating that He was equal with God the Father. The Jewish leaders just could not cope with His claims. In John 10:27-33 the Jews again observed that Jesus was claiming to be God. The Jews did not comprehend how a man could also be God. This claim by Jesus infuriated them to the point of wanting to stone Him. Looking back, I am amazed that the scribes and Pharisees could not figure out who He was. These religious leaders had studied all the prophecies about Messiah and His deity. When they actually looked at Jesus in His bodily form, however, they did not believe He was truly deity conceived by the Holy Spirit.

John 8:58 records a conversation in which Jesus referred to Himself as I AM. God was talking to Moses at the burning bush when He referred to Himself as I AM (Exodus 3:14). God's annunciation of His identity was something Moses never forgot. In John, when Jesus referred to Himself in the same manner as God did when He spoke at the burning bush, the conclusion is evident. He was claiming to be God! The unbelieving Jews of that era understood this claim, for in John 8:59 they attempted to stone Him for what they thought was blasphemy. Their hardened hearts and lack of spiritual understanding kept them from the truth.

In the Old Testament, God commanded the Israelites to offer blood sacrifices as payment for sin. He instructed the people that only animals without blemish qualified as a sacrifice. All animal sacrifices looked ahead to Jesus'

11

sacrifice. His offering, through death on the cross, ended all further need for restitution (Hebrews 10:12-14). Jesus was the sacrifice without blemish or spot (1 Peter 1:19). In order to be a spotless sacrifice He had to live a sinless human life (2 Corinthians 5:21). There is only one way someone could live a perfect life – He would have to be deity. The Bible states that Jesus lived a sinless life. In Hebrews 4:15 we read that Jesus "was in all *points* tempted as *we are, yet* without sin." Jesus is the only one that could have lived a sinless life. No other person in history has ever made the claim of living without committing any sin. This claim sets Him apart from all other religious leaders in history! Acts 20:28 states: "…church of God which He purchased with His own blood." When Jesus gave His life on the cross, His death would not have significance if He were a mere mortal. If he were mortal, He would have only been a martyr dying for a good cause. Only God, Himself, could be the perfect sacrifice that was the required payment for the sin of mankind. If God bought the church with His own blood, Jesus is the only One that could fulfill that statement and those previously quoted. Buying the church with His own blood as stated in Acts 20:28 verifies that Jesus was God.

Biblical Affirmation of Jesus' Deity

The Gospels note several incidents reaffirming Jesus' deity. In Mark 2:5-7 Jesus forgave the sins of the paralytic He was about to heal. The scribes reasoned in their hearts that He was blaspheming, because only God can forgive sins. They were partly right—forgiving sins is one of the prerogatives belonging only to God. Human beings forgive others in order to restore a strained or broken relationship. A simple mortal cannot restore another person's standing before God. Jesus was exercising divine authority in forgiving the man's sin or He was blaspheming.

Jesus exhibited power over nature. In Luke 8:22-24 we read that Jesus got into a boat with His disciples. When they encountered a windstorm so fierce that waves of water began to fill the boat, the disciples woke Jesus because they were terrified. In verse 24, Jesus spoke the word, the wind ceased, and the lake became calm immediately. This incident contributed to the disciples' initial understanding that Jesus was more than a mere mortal.

Matthew 14:22-33 relates the account of Jesus walking on water. Perhaps you have heard the statement: "If you think you are perfect, try walking on water." Walking on water demonstrated Jesus had power over nature – an attribute exclusive to God! Some might argue that Peter's walking on the water proved humans have abilities and powers that Jesus displayed. Careful reading of the passage reveals that Peter asked Jesus to command him to come to Him on the water. Peter was able to walk on the water only at Jesus' direction. If Peter had been able to walk on the water with his own ability, he would not have started sinking moments later when he took his eyes off Jesus and started focusing on the stormy waves. Additionally, he would have been able to regain his position on the waves and resume walking if he had the power within himself. It was not Peter's power that enabled this feat; he was depending entirely on Jesus' supernatural attribute!

Exodus 34:14 instructs God's people not to worship anyone but the Lord God. He is a jealous God and worshipping anyone or anything else is idolatry. In John 9:6-38 we find the story of a man blind from birth. Jesus restored his sight by putting clay on his eyes and directing him to go wash it off. In verses 35-38, the man whose sight was restored came back, wanting to know who Jesus was. When Jesus told him He was the Son of God, the man believed and worshipped Him. According to this account, Jesus received and approved of the man worshipping Him. No one knew the Scriptures better than Jesus did. The last command of the Bible is found in Revelations 22:9 where we are told to "Worship God." Jesus' response to the blind man leaves two possible conclusions: Either *He was a lunatic of epic proportion*, or, *He was God in the flesh!*

Finally, in John 2:18-22 Jesus made a prophetic statement that I believe was the most astounding prediction of all time! He prophesied that His body would be destroyed (crucified) but that in three days He would raise Himself from the dead! Think about it. Jesus stated He would rise from death by His own power. Undoubtedly, this was the most awesome display of power the world has ever witnessed. In today's world, an atomic bomb would be the biggest display of power ever known. Bombs are illustrations of the power to destroy; Jesus' display of power was to save lives! Jesus' statement was so amazing even the chief priests and Pharisees could not forget it. After Jesus' crucifixion, they went to Pilate asking for a secure watch on His tomb, because they remembered His prophecy in Matthew

27:63 that stated, "…Sir, we remember, while He was still alive, how that deceiver said, 'After three days I will rise.'" One of the best Scriptures for defending the deity of Christ is John 2:18. Jesus' claim of raising Himself from the dead does not contradict other passages where the Bible tells us God raised Him from the dead. Rather, these verses are in harmony with each other. The Father, Son, and Holy Spirit all participated in the resurrection of Jesus, and yet, any one of the three could have done it alone. The statement in John 2:18-22 and other Scriptures stating God raised Jesus from the dead are true with each standing on its own merit.

There is another example of this seeming contradiction. In Genesis 1:1 the Bible tells us God created the heavens and the earth. In John 1:3 and Colossians 1:16, the Bible says all things were made through Jesus. This may seem to be contradictory at first reading, but these verses are compatible in the same manner as those discussed above. Thus, the Father, Son, and Holy Spirit participated equally in creation and in Jesus' resurrection.

In John 10:17-18, Jesus spoke to the Pharisees about this issue. In verse 17, He stated that "I lay down my life that I may take it again." In verse 18, He explained further by saying, "I have power to lay it down, and I have power to take it again." Jesus was telling them that no one could take His life; He would lay it down. He also reminded them that He had power to take it again (raise Himself), just like He stated in the John 2:18-22 passage.

The Apostle Paul told Festus that Jesus "would be the first to rise from the dead" in Acts 26:23. We know this statement is not referring to numerical order. Several people were raised from the dead in Old Testament accounts. Jesus raised several people from the dead during His earthly ministry. By this we know Paul's statement had a deeper meaning. In I Corinthians 15:20-21 we read that "Christ is risen from the dead, *and* has become the firstfruits of those who have fallen asleep. For since by man *came* death, by Man also *came* the resurrection of the dead." Here we see Jesus is the first fruit. At the resurrection He did something significant that had never been done before. Jesus, the God Man, introduced the resurrection, starting with His own! He was the first, and only, person to raise Himself. He established the resurrection factor for all believers. In John 11:25 Jesus told Martha, "I am the resurrection and the life." In John 5:21-26 Jesus expounded even further on this subject. In verse 21 He stated, "For as the Father raises the dead and gives life to them, even so the Son gives life to whom He will." Here, Jesus told us that just as the Father has power to raise the dead, He also has the same power. Jesus can give life to anyone He wishes. There are no exception clauses in Jesus' statement in verse 21 or anywhere else. Power to raise "whoever He wills" means Jesus was able to raise Himself from the dead. In John 5:26 Jesus stated that "as the Father has life in Himself, so He has granted the Son to have life in Himself." Jesus had the same power over life and death, including His earthly life, as the Father does. Since Jesus lived on this earth as God, He obviously had the power to raise Himself from the dead.

Jesus told Philip in John 14:9, "He who has seen Me has seen the Father..." Philip most certainly had a hard time grasping the meaning of those words. It was difficult for all the disciples to comprehend that God could take on human form. Once again, the statement has only one logical conclusion. If Jesus was just a man or a created being, He could not have made that statement to Philip. It was another precise declaration of His deity. Jesus was God in the form of man on earth. He came to reveal Himself to humanity and to pay the required price for our sins. Anyone seeing Jesus while He was alive was seeing God. Some might argue that no one could see God and live. This statement is true in the sense that no one could see the full Shekinah glory of God and survive. A human being could not stand in the full presence of God's holiness and live. We must remember that Jesus was in a human body. Taking on human form required the partial hiding of His full glory. Veiling of His glory was another privilege that Jesus gave up during His earthly life (Philippians 2:7-8).

In Paul's epistles, we find the deity of Christ mentioned repeatedly. Paul often uses the terms Lord Jesus Christ, Lord Jesus, or Jesus Christ our Lord in his writings. In these passages, the Greek word for Lord is kurios, meaning "supreme in authority." The many references to the Lord Jesus Christ in the New Testament present another Biblical claim that there is no authority above Him. If someone is truly supreme in authority, there cannot be another higher than that person. It does not mean Jesus is over God; rather, that they are equal (John 5:18). Romans 10:9 tells us if we want to be saved, we must confess the Lord Jesus and acknowledge that He is supreme. Apart from believing in the deity of Christ, there is no salvation.

An encounter with zealous missionaries in the 1970s motivated me to always be prepared for defending the Gospel of Christ. One Saturday morning, two members of a cult knocked on my door. I was a very young and enthusiastic Christian, ready for an opportunity to share my faith. I opened the door and invited them in. The men began telling me about Jesus, presenting Him much differently than what I knew and believed Him to be. Although I knew they were wrong in their presentation of Him, I lacked the knowledge to refute their doctrine.

Thirty years have passed since that morning, yet too many Christians today have the same problem I had then. I pray the Lord uses this little book to help readers in two vital areas: First, to equip believers for defending the deity of Jesus effectively and second, to help seekers find the truth about Him. Any person wanting to share the Gospel must offer a strong defense of the deity of Christ.

Experts now estimate there are over 1,100 recognized cults and they all stumble at the deity of Christ. I have read many definitions of a cult. Most are wordy, complex and difficult to understand. All cults have particular nuances and are unique in some way. Many cults contain perversions and brainwashing purposely meant to draw people into deception from which it is difficult to break away. I have studied the main cults in depth and have a basic knowledge of most new ones. Since all share one common factor, defining them is easier than many think. This common distinction is the core of the Christian faith. My definition is simply this: *A cult is any religious organization that denies the deity of Christ.*

Most cults believe and teach that Jesus is a created being of some sort. Each has a little different twist, but generally, they share that conclusion. One of the most common passages used to teach this is Colossians 1:15-16. Verse 15 states that Jesus is the firstborn over all creation. The cults use this statement to teach that He is the highest creation of God. The term firstborn actually refers to a position of priority;

that Jesus is the chief over creation. Verse 16 gives clearer understanding. It states, "For by Him (meaning Jesus) all things were created that are in heaven and that are on earth." If Jesus is a created being, that statement cannot be true. If Jesus is a created being, then all things were not created through Him! The passage actually contradicts the cults' own teaching when interpreted for what it says. One must beware taking a verse out of context and twisting it into a false teaching.

The Bible tells us plainly that if we do not abide in the doctrine of Christ, we do not have God. We must have the correct understanding of who Jesus is, for if we do not, we do not know God! Since denying the deity of Christ is the central, common thread of all cults, distinguishing true believers from the false is uncomplicated. Although it can be determined easily, do not think it lacks importance. To the contrary, it is vitally necessary for me to know what my church believes. If I am uncertain, I need to ask for clarification. Should my spirit raise a red flag regarding the issue, I must investigate for myself. If I learn the leaders of my church do not believe that Jesus is God in the flesh, I have the responsibility to get out of it as quickly as I can! It is imperative to make the belief that Jesus is deity, God in the flesh, my number one criteria for selecting a church fellowship.

Chapter 2
Revelation of Jesus

To say that Jesus is the Almighty may well be the strongest statement in the Bible about His true identity. Jesus ascribed to Himself the same credentials as the Father.
He is the Beginning and the End. He has always existed and always will.
He is Almighty God!

Throughout the Bible we find references addressing the identity of Jesus. Some books of the Bible speak to this more than others. For much of my Christian life, I felt the Gospel of John was the New Testament book offering the most information on the deity of Christ. However, a recent study of mine on the book of Revelation provided so much more material on this topic. When people think about Revelation, prophecy is almost always what comes to mind.

This is a logical thought because prophecy and end-time happenings are usually the focus of studies on Revelation.

The book of Revelation says many powerful things about Jesus. The official title and purpose of the book is "The Revelation of Jesus Christ." We read that in the opening line of Revelation 1:1. In the original language the word Revelation means disclosure and manifestation. The book discloses how Jesus fits into end-time prophecy and provides specific details about future prophetic events. Revelation is also a manifestation of Jesus. It gives a clear and distinct picture and description of who He is. We will look at the passages in the book of Revelation that discuss this topic and see where it takes us.

Revelation 1:4-20 provides a lengthy description and commentary on the person of Christ, for one of the major goals of this book is to manifest Jesus. Verse five reminds us that Jesus was the firstborn from the dead and the one who washed us from our sins in His own blood. In verse seven we are told that Jesus is coming back. We know this refers to Jesus because the Scripture tells us about His being pierced at the cross (Zechariah 12:10-14, John 19:34). The Scriptures are also clear on the point that Jesus is the one who is coming back. In Matthew 24:30 Jesus Himself told His disciples that He was coming back on clouds. He spoke at length about His return and gave us that vivid picture of how He was coming back. In Revelation 19:11-16 we see even more details about His return. We know this is referring to Jesus because verse eleven tells us that this person's name was the "Word of God" (John 1:1, 14). He is coming back with power and great glory! Revelation 22:20 explicitly tells us that Jesus is the one that is coming. Titus 2:13 implores us to look "for the blessed hope and glorious appearing of our great God and Savior Jesus Christ."

Jesus refers to Himself as "the Alpha and the Omega" in verse eight. The verse closes by Jesus referring to Himself as "the Almighty."

To say that Jesus is "the Almighty" may well be the strongest statement in the Bible about His true identity. Here Jesus ascribed to Himself the same credentials as the Father. He is the "Beginning and the End." He has always existed and always will. He is Almighty God! Jesus is God the Son, the second person of the Trinity. Another affirmation is that verse eight tells us He is the one "who is to come"—Jesus is coming back.

In verse eleven Jesus again refers to Himself as "the Alpha and the Omega, the First and the Last." Jesus tells us in this verse that He will be speaking to the seven churches in chapters two and three.

Verses 13-18 provide a description of Jesus. Verse 13 refers to the described individual as "One like the Son of Man." Jesus referred to Himself as the Son of Man several times in the Gospels (Luke 9:26, 6:5, 12:10). Verse 13 also tells us this person is in the midst of the seven golden lampstands. Chapter two verse one states that the author is that person. Since we have established that Jesus is the writer of the seven letters to the churches, the person in verses 12-18 is Jesus! Verses 14-15 tell us this person had "eyes like a flame of fire" and "His feet were like fine brass." Revelation 2:18 tells us that these two traits belong to the Son of God!

In verse 18 we are told that this person was dead but now lives forever more. This obviously refers to the resurrection of Jesus (Luke 24:5-7, Matthew 28:5-6). The person who is speaking was crucified, but is now alive!

It is clear that verses four through eighteen are referring to Jesus. It is clear all the way through this passage. Twice Jesus was referred to as the one who is, and who was, and is to come (v. 4, 8). This statement refers to the fact that He always existed; He is eternal. It also refers to His death (was) and resurrection (is). This sentence also tells us that He is to come. Jesus is the one that Scripture says is coming back.

The first chapter's context reveals Jesus and establishes the fact that He is the one "who is who was and who is to come." Verse eight also boldly proclaims Jesus as Almighty God; He is equal with the Father (John 5:18).

Jesus closed out His letter to the church in Laodicea in a powerful way. In Revelation 3:21 He stated that "To him that overcomes I will grant to sit with Me on my throne…" Jesus is sitting on the throne right next to His Father on His throne. A throne is for the king, the supreme ruler. In olden days, no one but the king would dare sit on his throne; for another to do so would bring dire consequences. Sitting on the throne is symbolic of who is in charge; it is reserved for the supreme authority (king) alone. Jesus sitting on the throne represents the fact that He is in charge, He is God, and He is equal with God the Father. In Revelation 21:4-7 we again see Jesus on the throne. Verse six says the person on the throne is "the Alpha and the Omega, the Beginning and the End." We have already seen this statement refers to Jesus. In verse seven Jesus further stated that "He who overcomes shall inherit all things, and I will be his God!" This is yet another declaration of His deity!   Jesus is on the throne, a powerful statement indeed!

In Revelation 4:1 a voice like a trumpet spoke to John.   In Revelation 1:10 we see the same voice, as of a trumpet speaking.   We have already concluded that the context of the book of Revelation so far is Jesus.   In chapter four we can ascertain that Jesus is the one that spoke to John and took him to heaven to see the setting there.   It may have been a vision or it could be that John was actually taken to heaven.   It really does not matter how the Lord revealed this to John; what he saw is the important thing.   Verse two tells us that John saw a throne with one sitting on it.   As we read this passage we must remember the purpose of the book is to manifest Jesus.   The throne was surrounded by the twenty-four elders.   Most scholars believe this represents the church.   Verse eight shows four living creatures, each having six wings.   Who or what they are is not the issue; it is what they said that matters. They said "Holy, holy, holy, Lord God Almighty, Who was and is and is to come." The four living creatures were worshipping the one on the throne—the one who is who was and is to come. As we saw earlier (Rev. 1:4, 8) this statement is referring to Jesus. The statement of the four living creatures also includes the proclamation that Jesus is the Lord God Almighty! The four and twenty elders then fell down to worship Jesus.

In Revelation 5:8 we see the twenty four elders again fall down to worship the Lamb. This prompts the obvious question, "Who is the Lamb?" I Peter 1:19 refers to the blood of Christ as that of a lamb without blemish and without spot. This passage tells us that Jesus fulfilled the role of being the Passover lamb found in Exodus 12:1-11. The blood of the Passover lamb on the door posts was what God required so that the death angel would pass them by. This lamb had to be one without blemish (Exodus 12:5). John the Baptist referred to

Jesus in this way when he twice called Him the Lamb of God (John 1:29, 36). In verse 29, John stated that Jesus "takes away the sin of the world." This is the covering or payment that only the Passover lamb could fulfill. From the above Scriptures we know Jesus is the Passover lamb, the spotless Lamb of God. In Revelation 5:12 we see that the referenced Lamb was slain, again pointing to Jesus' sacrificial death and atonement for us. Revelation 7:14-17 also refers to tribulation martyrs as those made clean by the blood of the lamb. Verse 17 tells us that the Lamb "is in the midst of the throne," a statement of utmost prominence. In Revelation 21:14 the twelve apostles of the Lamb are mentioned. This is another reference to Jesus and the twelve disciples (apostles). It is very clear that the Lamb is referring to Jesus.

One might ask, "Why is this so important?" The Lamb is mentioned several times in this book and needs to be identified. This will clarify other verses in Revelation as well. In Revelation 5:8-13 it is important because we see the twenty-four elders and angels and living creatures were all giving worship to the Lamb. This is most significant. As pointed out in chapter one of this book, the Scripture commands us to worship no one but God. The elders, angels, and living creatures were all in heaven in their perfected state. Since we know they would not give worship to anyone but God, this ratifies the fact that the Lamb (Jesus) is God.

In Revelation 6:1-17 the seven seals were opened and revealed by the Lamb. The seals included several judgments upon the people that were still on the earth. After these judgments in verse 15, all the men of the earth hid themselves in caves and in the mountains. The passage in verses 16-17 stated: "Fall on us and hide us from the face of Him who sits on the throne (Jesus) and from the wrath of the Lamb! For the great day of His wrath has come, and who is able to stand?" The wrath of the Lamb has fallen and the people on earth saw it and realized its origin. The Lamb (Jesus) was exercising His office as Almighty God by pouring out judgment on sinful mankind.

In Revelation 11:15-18 the seventh angel of the trumpet judgments made a proclamation. He said in verse 15, "The kingdoms of this world have become the kingdoms of our Lord and of His Christ, and He shall reign forever and ever." In verses 16 and 17 the twenty-four elders worshipped God saying, "We give You thanks, O Lord God Almighty, the One who is and who was and who is to come." Here, it is again shown that they referred to "the One who is and who was and who is to come." They worshipped this person (Jesus) and called Him Almighty God! This is yet another ringing endorsement of His deity and that He is the Sovereign God! As the second person of the Trinity, He is equal with the Father! We have God the Father, God the Son (Jesus), and God the Holy Spirit. All three are God and function together in the Godhead on an equal basis.

In Revelation 15:1-4 we see another great annunciation. In verses one and two the Bible tells us that John saw another great sight. In these verses John saw believers who were living on the earth during the tribulation period of the whole earth. Verse two states that these saints of God were the ones who had victory over the beast (the Antichrist, the world ruler) and over his image. In verse three these Christians sang the song of Moses and of the Lamb. In Exodus 15:1-21 Moses and the children of Israel sang a song to the Lord. This song was right after the Lord parted the Red Sea and killed all of Pharaoh's army when the waters came back. Evidently, the song of Moses and the song of the Lamb were to the same being. We have already concluded that without question the Lamb is Jesus. So the tribulation saints were singing this song to the Lamb in verses three and four. The song begins with a powerful statement, "Great and marvelous are Your works, Lord God Almighty!" The Lamb is referred to as Lord God Almighty! This is yet another affirmation of the fact that Jesus (the Lamb) is in fact God Almighty.

This same Jesus is later referred to in verse three as King of the saints. He is our coming King. Verse four tells us that "all nations shall come and worship before You, For Your judgments have been manifested." In Philippians 2:9-11 we are told that God gave Jesus the name above every name, "that at the name of Jesus every knee should bow, of those in heaven, and of those on earth, and of those under the earth, and that every tongue should confess that Jesus Christ is Lord." This passage complements the song of the Lamb by telling us that someday everyone in heaven and on the earth will worship Jesus as Lord (supreme authority)! In Revelation 20:4 the Bible tells us that all saints who were on the earth during the tribulation will be ushered into the 1000 year reign of Christ. Zechariah 14:16-17 talks about all those that survive the last great battle. They will go to Jerusalem to worship the King, the Lord of hosts. Jesus will reign and rule at that time for 1,000 years on the earth!

Revelation 16:1-7 begins with the seven angels that will carry out the bowl judgments. These judgments are terrible plagues that will be poured out on the earth. The seven bowl judgments end in Revelation 16:21. This verse describes the most horrible hailstorm of all history, with "*each hailstone* about the weight of a talent." A talent was an ancient measure equivalent to approximately 110 pounds. Imagine what damage such a hailstorm will cause!

In Revelation 16:4, "the third angel poured out his bowl on the rivers and springs of water, and they became blood." In verses five and six, the angel made the following declaration: "You are righteous, O Lord, The One who is and who was and who is to be, Because you have judged these things. For they have shed the blood of saints and prophets, And You have given them blood to drink. For it is their just due." This declaration is made about the One who is and who was and who is to come. As we have seen previously, this is a statement referring to Jesus.

It also talks about Him judging these things (verse 5). In verse seven, the angel further states, "Even so, Lord God Almighty, true and righteous are Your judgments." This statement tells us more about "the One who is and who was and who is to come." It tells us that His judgments referred to in verse five were true and righteous. The angel also proclaims that the one referred to in verse five is the Lord God Almighty! Again, Jesus is called by this title. His deity and prominence is there for all to see!

Later in Revelation 16:12-16 we see the sixth angel pour out his bowl on the great river Euphrates. This river flows through modern day Iraq, and is significant in Bible prophecy. This river will dry up, thus making the way for the 200 million man army found in Revelation 9:14-16.

We also see in Revelation 16:13-14 that demonic forces were gathering the kings of the earth for the battle of that great day of God Almighty. Verse 16 tells us that the gathering place is called Armageddon. This is referring to

41

the last great battle where the forces of evil will all be wiped out by Jesus Himself. Jesus prophesied this in Luke 21:27 where He stated, "Then they will see the Son of Man coming in a cloud with power and great glory." Jesus told the disciples in that passage that He would be coming back to exhibit all His power over kings of the earth and the forces of evil. Revelation 17:8-14 talks about the beast (Antichrist) and all his kingdoms getting ready to make war with the Lamb (Jesus). The Lamb will win that battle according to verse 14. Later in Revelation 19:11-21 we see Jesus returning to wipe out the forces of the Antichrist (verses 19-20) and the rest of the kings who were gathered there (verse 21).

It is clear that Jesus is the one fighting that battle. Revelation 16:15 sheds more light on the issue. Right in the middle of Verses 14 and 16, which talk about the great battle of Almighty God being fought at Armageddon, we see Jesus stating, "Behold, I am coming as a thief." We know that is Jesus speaking for two reasons.

First of all, every passage in Revelation and the rest of the Bible talking about "coming back," is referring to Jesus. I think that has been sufficiently substantiated. Secondly, this book is the revelation or manifestation of Jesus. Every place where someone from the Godhead is speaking, we know it is Jesus. Now that we have established that Jesus is the one who fights the battle on that great day, we can come to another conclusion. Since He is the One referred to in Revelation 16:14, it is obvious that He is God Almighty.

We stated earlier that in Revelation 17:8-14 the Bible shows us the forces of the beast and His kingdoms getting ready to make war with the Lamb (Jesus). We also are told that the Lamb will overcome them, for He is Lord of lords and King of kings. There are two other places where we see this title given to Jesus (I Timothy 6:15, Revelation 19:16). Saying that Jesus is Lord of lords and King of kings is a powerful statement. The earth has seen kings come and go. Some were very powerful, ruling

43

over most of the known world at the time of their reign. Alexander the Great, the Roman Caesars, and Nebuchadnezzar (Babylonian empire) all ruled kingdoms covering most of the then known world. The past few hundred years have also seen several eminent rulers (kings). Napoleon, Hitler, Hirohito and all the different leaders of the British Empire in the 1800s come to mind. All these rulers exhibited an enormous amount of power in this world. Yet, we read that Jesus is the King above all kings. All these earthly kings that were mentioned pale in comparison to Jesus, for He is the King above every king. The subjects of these earthly kings had to bow the knee to their authority. All these kings will have to bow their knees at the feet of Jesus because He is the ultimate King! He is the ruler over the kings of the earth (Revelation 1:5).

Verse 14 reminds us that the Lamb (Jesus) is Lord of lords. We have previously discussed that the term Lord means supreme in authority. There are many earthly lords. In the middle ages there were noblemen who were given the title lord. They exercised a high level of leadership in their realms. Great Britain's ruling body is called the House of Lords. It is comprised of elected officials providing leadership for the government. I looked up the term lord in *Webster's Universal College Dictionary*. It had several definitions. The first meaning listed was "a person who has authority, control, or power over others." However, this was not the definition that really caught my eye. Definition number eight was "the Supreme Being, God." Number nine was "Jesus Christ." Think of it, *Webster's Universal College Dictionary* refers to the Godhead and the deity of Jesus! Jesus is "supreme authority" over all earthly lords. All earthly lords will someday bow their knees to the Lord Jesus! As King of kings and Lord of lords, Jesus is over all. There is no one above Him. Jesus and the Father reign equally!

In Revelation 19:5-10 John relates what he heard. In verse five he heard a voice coming from the throne. John then heard the voice of a great multitude saying in verse seven: "Let us be glad and rejoice and give Him glory, for the marriage of the Lamb has come, and His wife has made herself ready." The church is the wife of the Lamb (Jesus), as written in Revelation 21:9-10. Verse nine says, "Come, I will show you the bride, the Lamb's wife." Verse ten shows us the holy city of Jerusalem, which will house all believers for all eternity. Revelation 21:2 also states that the New Jerusalem was, "coming down out of heaven from God, prepared as a bride adorned for her husband." Revelation 21:24, 27 further clarify this point by stating, "And the nations of those who are saved shall walk in its light…" Verse 27 tells us that the only ones who can enter the New Jerusalem are "those who are written in the Lamb's Book of Life." This clearly tells us that only believers will inhabit that city. All believers from the beginning of time will be there.

The voice speaking from the throne in verse five, told John in Revelation 19:10 not to worship him. He told John, "See *that you do* not *do that!* I am your fellow servant, and of your brethren who have the testimony of Jesus. Worship God! For the testimony of Jesus is the spirit of prophecy." John was told not to worship him, but to worship God.

Revelation 19:6-10 is one continuous thought. The subject of this thought is obviously the Lamb (Jesus). By telling John to worship God, this angel was clearly pointing to Jesus. We see the phrase, "the testimony of Jesus," sandwiched around the command to worship God. Due to this fact, the voice from the throne was telling John to worship Jesus as God!

Revelation 19:11-21 tells us about the coming of Jesus at the Battle of Armageddon. We know it is Jesus for several reasons. In verse 12 this person's "eyes were like a flame of fire" just like we see in Revelation 1:14, 2:18. We previously explained that Revelation 1:14 was referring to Jesus and all seven letters to the churches were written by Jesus.

In Revelation 19:10 the person who is coming is called "The Word of God." We also know that "The Word of God" is a surname given to Jesus (John 1:1, 14).

Revelation 19:16 states that this person, "has on His robe and on His thigh a name written: KING OF KINGS AND LORD OF LORDS." We established earlier that this refers to Jesus. Verse 15 reveals why this is important. It refers to Jesus and states: "He Himself will rule them with a rod of iron. He Himself treads the winepress of the fierceness and wrath of Almighty God." Here we see that Jesus was exercising the office of Almighty God by carrying out the fierceness of His wrath upon all unbelievers (verses 18-21). The subject of this passage from verse eleven through the end of verse 21 is unmistakably Jesus. Verse 17 shows us an angel crying out to all the birds, "Come and gather together for the supper of the great God." Since the context of this passage is always Jesus, we know that "the supper of the great God" also refers to Him. Jesus once again is shown to be deity!

John was given a vision of the New Jerusalem in Revelation 21. The vision gives a vivid description of what the city will be like. Verses 3-6 provide another glimpse of the person of Jesus. In verses 3-4 John heard a loud voice from heaven saying, "Behold, the tabernacle of God is with men, and He will dwell with them, and they shall be His people. God Himself will be with them and be their God. And God will wipe away every tear from their eyes; there shall be no more death, nor sorrow, nor crying. There shall be no more pain, for the former things have passed away." The loud voice from heaven was speaking of the heavenly bliss that will emulate from the New Jerusalem, for nothing negative will be there.

In verse five we find the one who sat on the throne in 20:11 told John to, "Write, for these words are true and faithful." In verse six He went on to say "It is done! I am the Alpha and the Omega, the Beginning and the End." The person on the throne told John to write those things down and to let John know that it was done. Verse six is key, as it identifies the person on the throne. This person stated He was "the Alpha and Omega, the Beginning and the End." Several prior passages in Revelation reveal that this term always refers to Jesus. Jesus is the one on the throne in verse five. The first glimpse of the one on the throne is found in Revelation 20:11. Revelation 20:11-21:8 is all one continuous thought. The person on the throne is the same one all the way through those verses. This would bring us to one more conclusion. Since the one on the throne in 20:11 and 21:5 is obviously the same person, Jesus then, is the one on the great white throne. Jesus is the One administrating at the Great White Throne Judgment. Jesus is the throned One in 20:11 and 21:5, another endorsement of who He really is!

There are other Scriptures where we see Jesus on the throne, as well. In Revelation 22:1-3 we see two more references of this. In verse one he (one of the seven angels, Revelation 21:9) shows John "a pure river of water of life, clear as crystal, proceeding from the throne of God and of the Lamb." In verse three the angel also stated "there shall be no more curse, but the throne of God and of the Lamb shall be in it." The Lamb (Jesus) is on the throne in both verses where He reigns with God the Father. It is clear they are in union, they are equal, and they rule together.

We have already stated that Revelation 21 revealed what the New Jerusalem will be like. Verses 22-23 give more unique insight, for the angel told John "I saw no temple in it, for the Lord God Almighty and the Lamb are its temple. The city had no need of the sun or the moon to shine in it, for the glory of God illuminated it. The Lamb is its light." The New Jerusalem evidently has no need for a church (temple) because the Lord God Almighty and the Lamb fulfill that need. There will be no need to go to church to worship the Lord anymore, because we will see the Lord face to face. We will literally bow at His feet in worship. This is what every believer will do someday in the New Jerusalem. We also see in verse 23 that the city did not need the sun or moon for a source of light. It tells us that the "glory of God illuminated it." Artificial light of any kind will not be needed there. The light bill will be zero each month! The shekinah glory of God will provide the light. Here we see that God, Himself, will provide light for everyone. At the end of verse 23 we are given one more tidbit of information on this subject. It gets more specific about this illumination. Here we are told that "the Lamb is its light." Jesus, the Lamb of God, will light the New Jerusalem with the full essence of His glory. Since this verse tells us that the glory of God is the light source, it is obvious that the verse is telling us that Jesus is God.

In Revelation 22:6 the same angel continues by saying to John, "These words are faithful and true. And the Lord God of the holy prophets sent His angel to show His servants the things which must shortly take place." Here, the angel told John that the "Lord God" sent him to share these things. We know that the term Lord God is referring to Jesus. We know this for two reasons. First, Revelations 22:6-7 is one complete paragraph. The Lord God Himself speaks in verse seven saying, "Behold I am coming quickly!" It has already been established that statement refers exclusively to Jesus. This clarifies who is referred to by the term "Lord God" in verse six; it is referring to Jesus. Second, Revelation 22:16 gives more insight on who the Lord God is in verse six. In verse 16 Jesus tells us that He sent His angel to testify of all these things. Verse six tells us the Lord God sent His angel to show these things. It is apparent that Jesus and the Lord God are the same One. Jesus is the Lord God!

I trust this brief narrative on the book of Revelation has provided more insight into Jesus. As you recall, Revelation 1:1 stated the two purposes of the book are to show end-time events and to manifest or reveal Jesus. We have focused on the latter purpose.

I must confess something to you. In past years I considered the book of Revelation as strictly a prophetic book. Recently, I have been studying the deity of Jesus in the Scriptures. During this time I felt the Lord prompting me to go through the book of Revelation again. This time I did not read it for the prophetic information. Rather, I wanted to see how it revealed or manifested Jesus. I was amazed at what I found when focusing on the person of Jesus. Now I believe that the Revelation is clearly the most definitive book in the Bible on Jesus' identity.

Here is a quick review of what we found in the book of Revelation. In 5:8-9 Jesus was worshipped (only deity is to be worshipped). We are commanded to worship Jesus in 19:10. Five times we see Jesus on the throne as God (3:21, 7:17, 21:5, 22:1, and 22:3). In 20:11-14 Jesus sits on the throne and presides over the Great White Throne Judgment of God. Twice

Jesus is referred to as "King of kings and Lord of lords" (17:14, 19:16). We see Jesus executing the office and wrath of Almighty God in judgment (19:15). Jesus lights the New Jerusalem with His glory, the glory of God (21:22-23). In 1:8 Jesus is referred to as "the Almighty." Four times Jesus is called "Lord God Almighty" (4:8, 11:17, 15:3, and 16:7). He is called "God Almighty" in 16:14. Finally, Jesus was referred to as "Lord God" (22:6). This is how Jesus is revealed in the last book of the Bible. I find this to be a strong resume. Do you agree?

Chapter 3
Further Evidence

In II John nine we see just how important Jesus is. This Scripture tells us "Whoever transgresses and does not abide in the doctrine of Christ, does not have God."
Without a proper and complete understanding of who Jesus is, we do not know God. Knowing Jesus' true identity is not optional—it is imperative.

Jesus' claims of deity separate Him from all other religious leaders. Scorn for His claims arose early in His earthly ministry and persist to this day. The scribes and Pharisees were among the first groups to reject His declaration that He was God (Luke 5:21). Other religious, political and social groups of that time also rejected His claims. One of the most interesting accounts occurred at the time of His resurrection. In

Matthew 28:4-11 we find the account of the angelic announcement. Verse four declares, "...the guards shook for fear of him, and became like dead *men*" when they heard the angelic statement concerning Jesus, "...for He is risen, as He said." They heard the angel's pronouncement, and they knew that no one came and stole Jesus' body from the grave. Yet, verse eleven tells us some of the guards went into the city and reported to the Jewish leaders what had happened. Then, they accepted a bribe from the Jewish leaders to spread the lie that the disciples stole His body while they slept. This was probably one of the most conspicuous rejections of Jesus' claims in all of history. They were firsthand witnesses to the resurrection announcement and knew it was true. Yet, favor with the Jewish leaders and greed for money was more important to them than the truth. Regrettably, the spirit of the Roman guards continues to this day.

Rejection of Jesus' claims has continued throughout the centuries. Today, the secular world mocks His claims of deity. Believers should not be surprised, for the Bible states that those who do so have the spirit of Antichrist because of their unbelief (1 John 4:3). We definitely can expect the unbelieving world to reject His claims. However, there are other disappointments that are harder to accept.

Inside the church today, we see Jesus' claims attacked. Many of our liberal seminaries are sending out leaders denying the deity of Christ. Some protestant churches have pastors rejecting Jesus' divine claims. It is easy to understand why there is so much confusion in the world when the foundation of our faith is suffering attacks from within. In 2 Timothy 3:5 the Bible tells us to expect this, for many have a form of Godliness, but deny "the" ultimate power! These teachers are upfront and blatant in their rejection of Christ's deity. I am confident that leaders of the protestant reformation would groan in their graves if they could see what is happening today.

In II John verse nine we see how important this issue really is. Here the Scripture tells us, "Whoever transgresses and does not abide in the doctrine of Christ does not have God." Without a proper and complete understanding of who Jesus is, we do not know God. Knowing Jesus' true identity is not optional, it is imperative!

Jesus Claimed to be God

People denying the deity of Christ overlook His claims. The Bible shows in at least nine places where Jesus claimed to be God. In John 5:18 the Jews understood that Jesus was claiming to be equal with God. This assertion enraged them to the point of wanting to kill Him. In their judgment, it was blasphemy for a man to claim to be God (equal with God). In John 10:31-33 the Jews again understood that Jesus was claiming to be God and, "...took up stones again to stone Him." John 8:57-59 records a conversation between Jesus and the Jews. During this exchange Jesus referred to

Himself as I AM. In Exodus 3:14 God talked to Moses at the burning bush, identifying Himself as I AM. I AM is the name of God. Therefore, when the Jews heard Jesus make His claim of deity they threatened to stone him, but He escaped their rage.

In a previous chapter, I pointed out that Jesus claimed to be the Messiah or Christ, and several Old Testament passages prophesied that the messiah would be God. There are three places in the Gospels where Jesus claimed to be the Christ, thereby claiming to be deity. During Jesus' conversation with the woman at the well as recorded in John 4:25-26, she declared, "'I know that Messiah is coming' (who is called Christ)." Then Jesus declared, "I who speak to you am *He*." In Matthew 16:13-20 Jesus asked His disciples who people thought He was. After they named several religious teachers and prophets, Jesus asked directly who they thought He was. Peter stated, "You are the Christ..." Jesus responded, "Blessed are you, Simon Bar-Jonah, for flesh and blood has not revealed *this* to you, but My Father who is in heaven." Mark 14:61-62 relates the interrogation proceedings during the trial of Jesus prior to His crucifixion. In this account, the high priest, all the chief priests, the elders and teachers of the law came together. The high priest stood up before the entire group and began asking Jesus to answer false accusations that witnesses had just made against Him. Jesus remained silent and gave no answer. The chief priest again asked Jesus, "Are you the Christ?" Jesus simply responded by saying, "I am." After that statement, they condemned Jesus to death. Jesus knew before answering that would be their response. As we have read in several Scriptures, Jesus claimed to be the Christ to the woman at the well, to His disciples, and to the rulers of Israel!

In Mark 2:28 Jesus referred to Himself as Lord of the Sabbath. Jesus referred to Himself as "The Lord" in the Mark 11:1-3 passage. In the Sermon on the Mount, Jesus again referred to Himself as Lord in Matthew 7:21-23. In chapter one, we discussed the Greek word for the term Lord, which means "supreme in authority." This is an important distinction in these three passages. In each, Jesus referred to Himself as Lord, which means He told them He was the ultimate authority. If someone is the ultimate or supreme authority, there cannot be anyone or anything above him. This raises a very important question. If someone claims to be the supreme authority, who is he claiming to be? In the previous nine passages, Jesus made some powerful statements and claims. Claims of such magnitude make the choices much clearer. Jesus was indeed claiming to be Lord (supreme authority) which is another statement of deity. There cannot be any questions or uncertainty on this point. When someone claims a certain identity, as Jesus did, the claims are true or the person is a liar, for there is no middle ground.

The Gospels have very little written about Jesus prior to His earthly ministry and baptism. Other than during His infancy, the only passage referring to his childhood is Luke 2:42-49. In this account, we find Jesus in the temple talking with religious teachers. Even at that young age, a glimmer of His divine power is apparent. In verse 47, the teachers were amazed at His understanding and answers. For Jesus to have a good grasp of the Scriptures at that age does not initially seem unusual. John 7:15 provides more insight into the matter by declaring, "The Jews were amazed and asked, "How does this Man know letters, having never studied?" In this passage, the Jews expressed amazement when Jesus taught in the temple. They knew he had not been formally educated and, therefore, would not be able to read the scrolls. In their society, only the elite were able to afford or even obtain an education. Jesus' earthly parents were common, ordinary people. The Jews did not understand how Jesus could read and teach without obtaining some formal education (you cannot teach Scripture if you cannot read). Of course, this magnifies the account of Jesus conversing with the teachers in the temple at the age of twelve. The question is: How could

Jesus do that as a preteen without education? The only logical answer is that even at that early age, He was exercising divine power!

Many world religions believe that Jesus was just a good man and a prophet. Some individuals go even further. They believe that Jesus' earthly identity is secondary since we all believe in the same God. John 14:1-10 teaches differently. Jesus stated in verse one there is a difference between believing in God in heaven and believing in Him. In verse six, Jesus reminded Thomas that He was the only way to the Father. A correct knowledge of Jesus' earthly identity is imperative to knowing the Father. He told Philip in verse nine: "…He who has seen Me has seen the Father…" Jesus made a bold statement in verse ten that summarizes who He is: "Do you not believe that I am in the Father and the Father in Me? The words that I speak to you I do not speak on My own *authority*; but the Father who dwells in Me does the works." It is very clear in the Scriptures that anyone who does not believe in the deity of

Christ on earth is ultimately rejecting God! The scribes and Pharisees were looking for Messiah to come. They knew all the Old Testament prophecies about Him and that He would be deity. They were looking for the Christ and some even thought John the Baptist was the Messiah (Luke 3:15). Most of the scribes and Pharisees rejected Jesus' claims, resulting in His denouncing them for not believing. The religious leaders' knowledge and wisdom was for naught, because they denied that Jesus was Messiah (John 5:39-40). At first only two from their group, Nicodemus and Joseph of Arimathea, believed Jesus was the prophesied Messiah (John 19:38-39). It was not until after the resurrection that other religious leaders believed (Acts 6:7). Jesus' teaching is clear. If you reject His earthly claims of deity, you are lost. The issue of Jesus' identity on earth is paramount and no areas of negotiation exist. Any compromise on this issue is tinkering with the foundation of the faith.

Those who state that Jesus was just a man on earth overlook other critical evidence. There are several instances where Jesus displayed divine attributes and power. First, we know that only God has the ability to create (Colossians 1:15-16, John 1:1-3, Genesis 1:1-3). We also see that God, Jesus, and the Holy Spirit, who comprise the Holy Trinity, made everything that was made. The passages in Colossians and John state that the Godhead made everything. All three participated in creation: God the Father, God the Son, and God the Holy Spirit! This reaffirms that no angelic or human being has the power and ability to create. Some of you might be thinking that everybody knows that! Actually, emphasis on this point is very important.

Scripture records two examples where Jesus exhibited His creative power. John 2:1-9 relates the account of Jesus turning the water into wine at a wedding. In verse nine we read about "the water that was made wine..." The word *made* is the same word used in John 1:3, where it refers to all things being made through Jesus. We know that John 1:1-3 is referring to Jesus because in John 1:14 we are informed that "the Word became flesh and dwelt among us" on earth. The Greek word for both usages is *ginomai*, which means, "to cause to be." Here, Jesus exhibited the creative power that belongs only to God. No man anointed by the Holy Spirit has that power! We know that because Colossians 1:16 tells us that Jesus created all things in heaven and on earth. Nothing was created except through Him.

We find another account of Jesus exercising creative power in Luke 9:12-17. This time Jesus fed the multitude with five small loaves and two small fish. Verse 14 tells us five thousand men were in the group. It is safe to assume that women and children were also present. We cannot say with certainty, but some Bible scholars estimate at least eight to ten thousand people gathered to hear Jesus' teaching that day. This record describes Jesus feeding the group with the five loaves and two fish, and after all ate and were satisfied, "twelve baskets of the leftover fragments were taken up by them." This was undeniably a miracle, but even more than that! In *Webster's Universal College Dictionary*, the word create is defined as "to cause to come into being, as something unique." What Jesus did clearly fits that definition. He caused food to come into being and it surely was unique. Jesus clearly exhibited creative power in this passage, which is a prerogative belonging only to God!

Jesus exercised the divine attribute of omniscience, which is the ability to see all and know all. There are several passages where Jesus demonstrates this attribute of God. In John 4:46-53 Jesus healed the nobleman's son. The healing, however, is not the focus. When the man saw Jesus in Cana of Galilee (verse 46), his son was at Capernaum. Jesus healed the boy even though he was miles away from him, and told the father in verse 50, "Go your way; your son lives." The point is that Jesus had knowledge of the boy's healing even though He was not in his presence. The question is: How did Jesus know the man's son was healed if he was not there? There is only one legitimate answer: He was exercising His omniscience.

The Son of God demonstrated His omniscience in other cases as well. There are several passages stating that Jesus knew or perceived people's thoughts (Matthew 9:4, 12:25; Luke 5:22, 6:8). There have been cases in my life when someone told me they knew what I was thinking. The major difference in those situations was the individual, based on previous experience or information, anticipated what I might be thinking. That person felt he knew me well enough to predict my thoughts. In some instances, the individual was right, but even then it was anticipation, not actually knowing my thoughts. These passages teach that Jesus *knew* their thoughts! In John 6:64 the Bible tells us that "...Jesus knew from the beginning who they were who did not believe, and who would betray Him." Jesus knew what was in their hearts all along.

Jesus operated His omniscience by predicting or knowing the future. In John 18:4, we read that Jesus knew what was going to happen. He knew He would be tried and convicted. He knew He would stand before Pilate and Herod. In John 11:1-17 Jesus also demonstrated this attribute. In verse four He indicated that God was going to be glorified through Lazarus' sickness. He also knew that Lazarus was already dead before He got close to Bethany (verse 14).

Jesus predicted His future betrayal and crucifixion (Matthew 20:17-19, 16:21; Mark 10:32-34; Luke 9:22, 18:31-33). In these passages, Jesus was not exercising the office of prophet. Many Old Testament prophets foretold the future, but under a different scenario. Anytime a prophet was about to prophesy, the statement was always prefaced by "thus saith the Lord." This phrase meant they were speaking words God told them to say. It was God's power and omniscience that made their prophecy valid. Jesus never said, "thus saith the

Lord" before a prophetic statement, because *He was the Lord!*

Jesus demonstrated His sovereignty (supreme authority). In Matthew 10:1-42 and Luke 10:1-20 we find two separate accounts of Jesus commissioning a group of his followers for ministry. In Matthew 10:1 Jesus met with His twelve disciples to prepare them for their ministry travels. We read that Jesus gave them power over unclean spirits, sicknesses and diseases. In Luke 10:1, Jesus commissioned seventy of His followers to go out for ministry. Jesus instructed them to go to every city that He was planning to visit. They returned rejoicing because the demons were subject to them in Jesus' name. In the Matthew passage, the power to heal evidenced Jesus' authority. In the Luke passage the seventy rejoiced because they had power over demons in Jesus' name. It is clear that Jesus' disciples and followers could not have done anything without His authority. The only accounts of the disciples healing sicknesses or casting out demons are the two previously mentioned occasions. In Matthew 17:14-21 the disciples could not cast out the demon, for they did not receive that power from God on a consistent basis until after Pentecost. The point here is that only God can give that power. If Jesus was just a man operating under the power of the Holy Spirit, He could not have given His disciples power over unclean spirits, sicknesses and diseases. Otherwise, every believer today under the power of the Holy Spirit could pass out that power to others with a 100% guarantee that they would be able to perform any miracle they deemed necessary. We know this is not the case. In these two passages, Jesus gave His sovereign authority over demons and sicknesses to select followers. There is no evidence that any of the commissioned believers had less than 100% success. Luke 10:17 tells us that all seventy returned with joy because they had complete success on what Jesus sent them to do. Jesus exercised His authority as God in human form by giving power over demons and diseases to the disciples and followers. This type of power can only be commissioned by deity.

We have already discussed other demonstrations of Jesus' deity on earth. Jesus exercised power over nature (Matthew 14:33, Luke 8:24), and lived a sinless human life (Hebrew 4:15, 2 Corinthians 5:21), something only God can do!

Previously, we mentioned that Jesus forgave sins (Mark 2:5-7). If He had only been a man living under the power of the Holy Spirit, that would be blasphemy! He received and approved of others worshipping Him (John 9:35-38). This also would be blasphemy if He were just a man! Forgiving sins and receiving and approving of others worshipping you, are prerogatives belonging only to God. Last of all, Jesus predicted He would raise Himself from the dead! No mortal would dare make a statement like that, or be able to deliver on such a promise. As you can see, the Bible is clear: *When Jesus walked this earth, He was God taking on human form.*

Jesus exercised His divine attributes while He was on earth. The only attribute He did not exercise was omnipresence, because His humanity made that impossible. Every other attribute of God was displayed by Jesus.

Several years ago, I met with a young man in the local county jail. We were talking about the differences between the Bible and the Quran. Initially, he stated they complemented each other. To this opinion, I pointed out the major difference between the two teachings, which is Jesus' deity. The Quran presents Jesus as only a good man and a prophet. We talked at length about that issue. At the end of our conversation, we agreed on two major points. First, we agreed the identity of Jesus is the major difference between our beliefs. Second, we agreed that only one of us can be right. Jesus is the most important issue of the faith. Knowing His true earthly identity is imperative.

Chapter 4
Practical Evidence

Science, archaeology, and history continue validating the Biblical account of events.

The past three chapters were dedicated to showing the Biblical proof of the deity of Christ. I understand this may not be enough for some. The next line of debate for skeptics is usually attacking the truth and accuracy of the Bible. Critics often claim the Bible has been changed, or is just a mythical book. If the Bible is God's Word, there should be corroborating facts. This chapter will focus on practical evidence. If Jesus is deity, there should be historical facts supporting that, as well. If the truth can be proven by faith only, the case will seem weak to some skeptics. Truth, however, stands up to every test. Obviously, if it cannot do that, it will not be the truth. Let us now look at facts substantiating the premise of the previous three chapters. We will examine historical information and validate some Biblical accounts many unbelievers bring into question. We will demonstrate proof of Scriptural soundness, its accuracy, and that none of its meaning has been lost over the last two millenniums. If the data and accounts of the Scripture can be verified, we have a solid basis of truth. Now, let us examine information everyone can access and see where it leads.

Josephus

Josephus has long been regarded as one of the main Jewish historians of the first century. Many around the world who have varying backgrounds and mindsets accept his writings. Charles Pfeiffer wrote an account of Josephus' background in the foreword of *The Works of Josephus* volume I. He stated that Josephus was born in approximately 37 A.D. He was well educated in Jewish and Greek culture. Josephus spent quite a few years in Rome trying to teach them about Jewish traditions:

> It was during his time in Rome that he wrote the historical accounts that now make him famous. This unique balance of Roman and Jewish culture help validate his writings. He had no bias. In fact, Rome may have had the greater influence in his life. Rome had a great empire and a great history. It was there that he learned the importance and significance of the factual side of history.[1]

In 1752, William Whiston of Cambridge, England, made and published the standard English translation of the works of Josephus. In the appendix, he also included a list of fifteen historians that had quoted Josephus on various historical facts. The first historian was in the first century and others continued up until Mr.

Whiston's generation. Josephus' credentials have passed the test of time.

We mention this fact because of one paragraph that Josephus wrote about Jesus. The following is his account:

> Now, there was about this time Jesus, a wise man, if it be lawful to call him a man, for he was a doer of wonderful works—a teacher of such men as receive the truth with pleasure. He drew over to him both many of the Jews, and many of the Gentiles (non-Jews). He was the Christ; and when Pilate at the suggestion of the principal men amongst us, had condemned him to the cross, those that loved him at the first did not forsake him, for he appeared to them alive again the third day, as the divine prophets had foretold these and ten thousand other wonderful things concerning him; and the tribe of Christians, so named from him, are not extinct at this day.[2]

These are the comments of the primary Jewish historian of the first century. Several of the twelve apostles were still alive during Josephus' life, as well as many other followers of Jesus who were eye witnesses of His life. Initially, Josephus refers to Jesus' humanity. He was an historical figure. He stated Jesus was the Christ! Remember, we previously discussed that topic. The terms Christ and Messiah were synonymous in the Jewish culture. The Messiah was foretold to be deity by the Old Testament prophets. Josephus knew what the prophets said about the Messiah. In fact, he refers to them in his statement on Jesus. He was plainly stating that Jesus was the Christ, which as we discussed, means that He was God in the flesh! He also referred to the cross and that Jesus rose again the third day. The resurrection was God's final stamp of approval. It showed to mankind that Jesus was who He said He was! He referred to many other things (10,000) the prophets foretold and Jesus fulfilled. Josephus, one of the prominent historians of the first century, bears out the claims of Jesus. Two things about Jesus are questioned the most: His deity and His resurrection. Josephus confirms both! We must remember the influence Rome had on the thinking of Josephus. Christians were heavily persecuted during the time he was in Rome. It is inconceivable that he would have written his statement about Jesus unless he knew it to be a fact, for no person would put his neck on the chopping block for a myth!

Josephus wrote on many other areas of the Bible at which unbelievers scoff. Noah's Ark was a major topic of his writings. In Genesis 6:1-9:17 we find the Biblical account of Noah and his building of the ark. This account begins with the wickedness of men during that time. The Bible tells us in 6:5-12 how man's evil deeds made the earth corrupt and that God was sorry that He had put man on the earth. God decided to bring a worldwide flood to destroy mankind. Noah and his family were the only righteous people on the earth at that time and

God decided to spare them from the flood. God instructed Noah to build an ark to preserve his family from the flood that was to come (6:13-17). God also told Noah to bring animals onto the ark (6:19-20). The Lord then sent the rains that continued for forty days and nights nonstop (Genesis 7:4), and the waters covered the mountains (Genesis 7:20). We thus know that every living thing was destroyed (Genesis 7:21-22), since the water covered the whole earth. For the waters to cover the mountains, it is evident the flood was worldwide. The Bible account also tells us that Noah's ark came to rest in the mountains of Ararat. This area is found in present day Turkey. The story of Noah's ark and the worldwide flood has been ridiculed by many. It is referred to as a myth or a fairy tale by the unbelieving world.

In Josephus' comments concerning Noah's Ark, he states the account of the Bible and where the ark landed, and then he makes a remarkable statement. He wrote that:

...the Armenians call this place *The Place of Descent*, for the ark being saved in that place, its remains are shown there by the inhabitants to this day.[3]

Josephus wrote that during his time the remains of the ark were still visible. Here again, we see the prominent first century historian verify an account of the Bible that many refuse to believe. This is a powerful affirmation of the Scriptures!

Another Biblical account that some people scorn is the destruction of Sodom and Gomorrah. In Genesis 19:1-29 we read the account of God's overthrow of those two cities. Sodom and Gomorrah were judged for their wickedness. In Genesis 18:20 God states that the outcry against the two cities is great and their sin is grave. God saved only Lot, his wife, and his two daughters (Genesis 19:15) from the coming calamity. In Genesis 19:24 we read that God rained fire and brimstone on Sodom and Gomorrah until the cities were burned to the ground. (Genesis 19:27-28). The smoke was like that of a huge furnace, destroying everyone and everything there. In Genesis 19:26, we are told that Lot's wife was turned into a pillar of salt for disobeying the command in Genesis 19:17.

Following is a portion of Josephus' report on this Biblical account:

> ...it was of old a most happy land both for the fruits it bore and the riches of its cities, although it be now all burnt up. It is related how, for the impiety of its inhabitants, it was burnt by lightning; in consequence of which there are still the remainders of that divine fire; and the traces of the five cities are still to be seen, as well as the ashes growing in their fruits.[4]

Josephus described in detail the devastation from Sodom and Gomorrah that was still evident during the first century A.D.! Most scholars acknowledge that Sodom and Gomorrah were destroyed 2,000 years before Josephus' time. The fact that the evidence was still there shows how complete and how devastating the destruction really was. The fact that the prominent first century historian reported that the evidence was still there, is a ringing endorsement of the Biblical account! In his writings, Josephus also refers to the calamity of Lot's wife. He writes that:

> But Lot's wife continually turning back to view the city as she went from it, and being too nicely inquisitive what would become of it, although God had forbidden her to so do, was changed into a pillar of salt; for I have seen it, and it remains at this day.[5]

Josephus states that he had seen the pillar of salt with his own two eyes. Salt does not appear in that form or manner naturally. It could only have occurred by divine intervention, and we have a noted historian who was an eyewitness to the fact that the pillar of salt was still there.

In conclusion, we have the statements of Josephus on Jesus, Noah's Ark, Sodom and Gomorrah, and Lot's wife. His accounts clearly validate all four! We must remember that Josephus did all his writing while he was in Rome. He was considered a traitor by the Jews because he went to Rome and adopted the Roman way of life. In the first century, history tells us how hard Rome was on Christianity. Christians were thrown to the lions and their dead bodies were often used as torches to light the city. It is important to remember that Josephus lived in first century Rome when he wrote *The Works of Josephus*. We can see that Josephus' commitment to the facts would be the only reason for validating Christianity, and thereby, jeopardizing his own future. Here we see strong evidence to sustain Jesus' claims and three other important Biblical events!

Dinosaurs

Critics attack the Bible (and Jesus) in another area, by saying it is out of touch with reality. They declare the Bible does not address main issues that science deems significant. One argument asks why the Bible does not talk about dinosaurs. It states the Bible is obviously irrelevant in the scientific arena because it ignores that issue. No one questions whether or not dinosaurs existed, for the fossil records show proof over and over again. Their position is that since the Bible is silent on this important issue, it is out of touch with scientific facts that are known to be true. As a result, they have other questions disputing whether the Bible is relevant in any area.

The problem with the above argument is that the Bible does refer to dinosaurs. In Job 40:15-24 we find God reminding Job about behemoth. That animal was contemporary with Job; otherwise, he would not have known what God was talking about. God would not bother to talk about an animal of which Job had no knowledge. In the original language, behemoth refers to "large animal." Some translators state this may be an elephant or hippopotamus. As we examine the Biblical account, we see that cannot be true. Have you ever seen the tail of either of these animals? Both have fairly short spindly tails. In verse 17, Scripture tells us that this animal had a tail like a cedar! There is only one animal that ever had a tail to fit that description — the dinosaur. Verse 19 goes on to tell us this animal is, "the first of the ways of God" — the largest of His creation! No one questions that dinosaurs were the largest animals ever to walk the earth. This passage of Scripture clearly declares that dinosaurs existed and were contemporary with man.

Dead Sea Scrolls

Another leading argument against the authority of Scripture is the claim that man has corrupted the translation over the past 2000 years.   The contention is that whether intentional or unintentional, the Scriptures have been polluted through man's translations. The implications are great. If man has contaminated the Scriptures, then it really is not God's Word. If there is not definite assurance of Scriptural truth, then it is just a good book to read, but not the words of God to us.

Many consider the Dead Sea Scrolls to be the greatest archaeological find of the twentieth century: In his book, *The Dead Sea Scrolls Today*, James C. VanderKam wrote about this great archaeological find.

He stated that the scrolls were discovered in a cave near the Dead Sea in 1947. The scrolls were found to be a copy of the book of Isaiah in the Old Testament of the Bible. Paleography was used to establish when the scrolls were written. Paleography is the study of ancient scripts and the ways letters were shaped by scribes when writing or copying texts. Styles of letter formation change over time, which enables paleographers to determine the era in which scripts were written. This study showed the scrolls were probably written in the first century B.C. The scrolls were checked for accuracy by expert scholars. They found the Dead Sea Scrolls and the current book of Isaiah are almost identical. Only slight points rarely altering the text's meaning were found. The Isaiah scroll reveals that the Scriptures have not changed through translations since the time of Christ. Carbon-14 dating was another test used to determine the age of the scrolls. This analysis placed the writing of the scrolls to be around the time of Christ's birth.[6]

The Dead Sea Scrolls are considered the greatest find of the twentieth century because they reveal that the Scriptures remain accurate, to the dismay of skeptics. They silence that criticism and show God has sovereignly protected His Word so that His truth can be made known to all generations! What all believers have stood on for generations is now an established archaeological and historical fact!

Finding the Book of Isaiah is even more significant than finding the Dead Sea Scrolls, I believe. We have already discussed that in Isaiah 7:14 and 9:6-7, Jesus' deity was foretold. The Dead Sea Scrolls verify the fact that these prophecies were made hundreds of years before Christ was born. No one can now say the Scriptures are not accurate and true. This archaeological find verifies both! I encourage you to read more of Mr. VanderKam's writings. The Dead Sea Scrolls may well be the most important archaeological find in modern history.

Creation vs. Evolution

The debate between creationists and evolutionists has been long and arduous. The battle is often passionate as the discussion rages on. Scientists are learning more every year as research intensifies and they obtain more data. The evolutionary argument is simple in some ways, yet complex in others. I believe there are three foremost components to the evolutionist's argument, with everything else flowing from them. First, evolutionists believe the earth is several million years old. The earth's age is a key component to their argument. Second, evolutionists believe the big bang theory. They say everything came from a big explosion of matter several million years ago. Third, evolutionists believe that life was produced from nonliving matter.

Scientists continue finding information that supports the creation theory. It is exciting to me that many scientists now are supporters of the Genesis account. The creation account is very simple. In the first chapter of Genesis we read that God created everything in six days. The best commentary that I have read on this debate is written by Dennis R. Petersen. In his book, *Unlocking the Mysteries of Creation,* Petersen makes some powerful arguments for the Biblical account, along with key rebuttals of the evolutionary stance. The key issues listed below are addressed in his book:

> Mr. Peterson discusses the big bang theory, and asks the interesting question, "Do explosions create order or chaos?" The answer to that question should be obvious.

> He also comments on the earth's age. If the earth is several million years old, it would create a serious problem for evolutionists. If Adam and Eve were on the earth millions of years ago, the natural exponential growth of the earth's population would be astronomical. The earth would not be able to support that big of a population. Total population would be many times greater than the six billion plus the earth now contains.

Another fallacy of the evolutionary model is that random chance produces all the complexity of living things. The human skeleton has about 200 bones. What are the odds of 200 bones randomly being put together in the right order? It would be the number ten with 375 zeros behind it, to 1. Sheer numbers show the impossibility of this occurring by accident.

Dennis Petersen has a lot more information on the scientific proof for a young earth as opposed to the "millions of years" theory that evolutionists put forward. He also shows the fallacy of the big bang theory. Explosions never cause order; rather, they only produce chaos. Energy cannot produce life and the statistical improbability of the evolutionary theory of how life began and evolved is astounding.[7]

I trust these selected arguments from Dennis Peterson's book will whet your appetite to learn even more. Remember, God is a God of order; His truth is based on the facts. It would not be the truth if it were not so! Evolutionists often state that it takes too much faith to believe God created everything. It requires a lot more faith to believe the evolutionary theory over the Biblical account. Dennis Petersen clearly demonstrates the huge problems that evolutionists cannot answer. The more scientists probe with open minds, the more the Scriptures are proven to be accurately written evidence of historical events.

Long Life

Genesis chapter five talks about the earth being populated and records brief accounts of life spans. In verse five we are told that Adam was 930-years-old when he died. Verse eight states Seth died at the age of 912. Genesis 5:11-31 lists the ages of several other men: Enosh, 915; Cainan, 910; Mahalalel, 895; Jared, 962;

Methusaleh, 969; and Lamech, 777. Skeptics look at these extremely long ages and cite them as making the Bible unbelievable.

Dr. Carl Baugh writes about the accounts of long life that are recorded in the Bible in his excellent book, *Panorama of Creation*. Dr. Baugh is the founder and director of Creation Evidences Museum in Glen Rose, Texas. Dr. Baugh is known internationally as a minister and special creation speaker. In addition to degrees in theology, he holds a master's degree in archaeology and a Ph.D. in education, both from Pacific College of Graduate Studies. When he was in school he accepted the premise of evolution, but afterward came to the conclusion that only the creation account in the Bible held the answers to life on earth. The following are notable conditions of the earth's pre-flood environment explored in his book:

> Dr. Baugh writes that the earth was initially covered with a canopy which filtered out all the harmful things from

the earth. He goes on to state that this canopy produced optimum living conditions for plants, animals, and humans. Dr. Baugh goes into detail describing this canopy and found that those conditions could possibly create an amazing environment: Bigger plants, bigger animals, and bigger humans. He found that these conditions would also lead to longer life.[8]

I encourage everyone to visit the Creation Evidences Museum. My wife and I have visited several times, taking in the video presentation and viewing the hyperbaric chamber on exhibit in the museum. The hyperbaric chamber already shows that insects live longer and grow larger under those conditions. Dr. Baugh is presently constructing the world's first hyperbaric biosphere. The purpose for both is simulating pre-flood conditions. Once Dr. Baugh has conclusive evidence, we might have scientific proof to validate the long ages of mankind found in Genesis chapter five.

Die for a Lie?

We get our information from the past through history books and eye witness accounts. For information to stand up to scrutiny, the credibility of the eyewitnesses is primary. In many ways, the Bible is history and the men writing the New Testament need to pass the credibility test. Apostles of the Lord wrote all but two or three books in the New Testament (Hebrews, Luke and Acts). We then need to determine a good formula for their reliability.

Josh McDowell writes in his book, *More Than a Carpenter*, that almost all of the apostles were martyred:

1. Peter   crucified
2. Andrew   crucified
3. Matthew   the sword
4. John   natural

5. James, son of Alphaeus   crucified
6. Philip   crucified
7. Simon   crucified
8. Thaddaeus   by arrows
9. James, brother of Jesus   stoned
10. Thomas   spear thrust
11. Bartholomew   crucified
12. James, son of Zebedee   the sword[9]

The key to this issue is what happened after the crucifixion of Jesus. There are two different accounts. The Roman guards spread the story that the disciples stole Jesus' body from the tomb (Matthew 28:11-15). The apostles' account was that Jesus had indeed risen from the dead. The truth on this subject is critical. If the resurrection were a hoax, what would the result have been? Undoubtedly, the disciples would all have returned to their fishing nets, tax business, or whatever they could find. Their message would have died at that time. Remember, Jesus prophesied that he would rise from the dead after three days (John 2:18-22).

If He did not rise on the third day, then He would be a false prophet and a charlatan. The disciples, above all people, knew the truth about the resurrection. There are several accounts in the Gospels regarding Jesus appearing to the disciples after His resurrection (Mark 16:14, Luke 24:36-43, John 20:19-23, John 20:27-29, John 21:1-18). If Jesus had not risen from the dead, the disciples would have been the primary ones to verify it. Yet, as previously noted, they gave their lives for this same Jesus!

The ultimate question is: Would these men give their lives for a lie? Some might respond that many have done so and that many will still do so. This is true, but no one would die for something they knew was a lie. It would have been impossible for the disciples to be deceived about this since Jesus appeared to them several times. The disciples would have been the foremost witnesses to the fact that Jesus had risen from the dead, for they saw him face to face. If Jesus had not risen, the disciples would have gone back to their secular jobs. If Jesus had not risen, the movement would have lost its hope and therefore, would have faded away as others have throughout history.

Many people living then believed the report of the Roman guards, and many still do to this day. At that time, it was a death penalty offense when a Roman guard's watch was broken through prisoner escape or otherwise. Earlier in the book we talked about the guards being bribed by the Pharisees and receiving assurance that they would take care of things with their Roman supervisors. How do you think the guards would have handled the situation if that provision had not been granted? Would they have reported to their superiors that someone stole Jesus' body and risk the consequence of death? That is unlikely. They would not have intentionally chosen to die for something that was a lie!

The same reasoning applies to the apostles. The greatest proof of the authenticity of the Gospel may well be the apostles offering their lives for the message of Jesus.

Summary

I appreciate the continuing growth of information being compiled that substantiates the truth and accuracy of the Scriptures. We have just discussed different research projects conducted by experts with various professional backgrounds. We have shared evidence from a noted historian, scientists, and eyewitness accounts. The historian Josephus has provided factual evidence for the divine claims of Jesus. He also confirms the accounts of Noah's Ark and Sodom and Gomorrah. Many scientists now agree it is easier to believe the creation account than it is to believe the theory of evolution. Researchers are documenting scientific evidence that supports the long life spans in the pre-flood era. The Dead Sea Scrolls provide documented proof that the Bible is accurate and nothing has been changed over the past 2000 years. Last of all, we can read eyewitness accounts verifying the Biblical account of Jesus.

As we began this chapter, the goal was to verify the reliability and exactness of the Scriptures. A lot of information and evidence has been presented for your careful consideration. The question now is: What do you think?

Notes

1. William Whiston, *The Works of Josephus,* Volume I (Grand Rapids: Baker Book House, 1984) vii.

2. Ibid, Volume IV. 11.

3. Ibid, Volume II. 76.

4. Ibid, Volume I. 331.

5. Ibid, Volume II. 93.

6. James C. VanderKam, *The Dead Sea Scrolls Today* (Grand Rapids: William B Eerdmans

Publishing Company, 1994) 3, 16-20, 123-126.

7. Dennis R Petersen, *Unlocking the Mysteries of Creation* (El Dorado: Creation Resource Publications, 2002) 76-96.

8. Carl E Baugh, *Panorama of Creation* (Oklahoma City: Hearthstone Publishing, Ltd, 1992) 54-58.

9. Josh McDowell, *More Than a Carpenter* (Wheaton: Tyndale House Publishers, 1977) 61.

Chapter 5
Final Arguments

So what should I do with the evidence?

This completes our discussion about the claims of Christ and the accuracy of the Scriptures. I realize some individuals will still resist. For those skeptics, the last arguments are probably 1) they do not believe a loving God would send someone to hell, or 2) there is no hell.

Let us explore the hypothetical illustrations on the practical application of these two arguments. If you believe a loving God would not send a person to hell, you would then believe that everyone will go to heaven. If all are going to heaven, there is no accountability for what a person does on earth, and every murderer, rapist, terrorist, etc., will enter the pearly gates. How many people would look forward to heaven if that is true? Heaven would be no different from this earth, if all are going there. This belief simply does not make logical sense. One would be free to do anything, no matter how evil, because eternal penalty against wicked personal actions would not exist. Yes, there would be consequences from man, but those would be temporary and in some cases, even arbitrary. Mankind could live by a different set of rules if there were no eternal accountability. I believe heaven would lose its appeal to most folks if everyone is going there.

Some people believe this earth is hell. Undisputedly, this earth is full of wickedness and evil people. As long as sinful mankind lives on the earth, that will not change. If everyone on earth is going to heaven, however, its attractiveness is definitely diminished.

Some people believe hell really refers to annihilation. This belief states that when death occurs, life comes to a sudden and certain end of existence. Annihilation requires Biblical passages mentioning hell to be taken figuratively, rather than literally. One of the cardinal rules of interpreting the Bible is this: Always take a passage literally, unless there is strong evidence against doing so. The context of a passage always determines whether it is figurative or not. For example, many passages in Revelation are not to be taken literally. In those passages, it is usually apparent the verses could not be taken literally, because they would not make sense.

In the Scriptures, the case for hell is even stronger. The Bible speaks of hell in many different places and Jesus spoke about hell frequently. In fact, the majority of passages about hell in the New Testament are found in the Gospels. As we look at the Scriptures discussing hell, we find some notable information. In Luke 12:5, Jesus stated that they should only fear Him that had power to cast them into hell. The term "cast" implies that someone must take action to send a person there. This is a reminder that God has the final authority to send someone to hell. It also states that God is active in the process of what happens after death.

The following Scriptures speak about hell fire: Matthew 5:22, Matthew 18:9 and Luke 16:24. The Scripture tells us this fire is everlasting in Matthew 18:8 and 25:41. Everlasting fire obviously shows that life continues after death and there are eternal consequences. Physical bodies will die, but spiritual bodies will not be consumed in the fire of hell. Spiritual bodies will live in hell forever, if that is their eternal destiny. To illustrate what hell will be like, let us suppose someone built a fire in an enclosed area. When the fire was established, you were thrown into the fire: You could not get out of the fire due to the enclosure, and you could not die. This is a horrific scene to consider, but it is a picture of what hell will be like. Hell is the eternal place where fire and torment never cease.

As we understand this concept, the words of Jesus in Matthew 13:42 come into sharper focus. Hell's eternal torment will cause wailing and gnashing of teeth. Wailing usually consists of someone going through extreme emotional pain. A woman sobbing uncontrollably at the funeral of her child is an example. Overcome with grief, this woman cannot be consoled. When a person finds that he is in a fiery eternal hell, he will have good reason to wail! Gnashing of teeth occurs when someone is experiencing extreme physical pain. Bumping a knee or elbow on a sharp object often causes intense pain. When this happens, the person clenches his teeth during the brief time pain is at its peak. Once a person realizes he is sentenced to the torment of hell forever, there will be continual gnashing of teeth. Now we can understand why Jesus spoke about hell so often. He wanted to warn every one of its eternal torment and suffering.

The most descriptive passage on hell is Luke 16:19-31. In this passage we read about the rich man in hell as he cried out for mercy (v. 23-24). These verses reveal the rich man still had all of his senses. In verse 23, he could see; in verse

24, he could feel and taste; and in verse 25, he could hear. This passage clearly relates the consciousness and torment that all who are condemned to hell will experience. Some argue that this passage is a parable and not to be taken literally. The answer to that is easily explained. None of Jesus' parables ever included the specific name of an individual. Lazarus (v. 20), Moses (v. 31), and Abraham (v. 30) are all named in this account by Luke.

Many say a God of love would not send people to hell. Indeed, God is love, for the Scriptures repeatedly state that fact. However, the Bible also teaches that God is fully just. The Word of God commands those that love the Lord to hate evil (Proverbs 8:13, Psalms 97:10). The Bible states God hates sin so much that He considers it an abomination. In fact, that is why God had to turn His back on His own Son while Jesus was bearing the sin of the whole world (Matthew 27:46). Jesus was aware that the Father had turned His back on Him when He cried out in agony, "…why have you forsaken me?" Romans 3:10-18 tells us how God views mankind. These verses proclaim that no one is righteous, all are unprofitable, and no one does good. This clearly shows the high standard of God. He is total righteousness and anything less than that is unacceptable in His eyes. Isaiah 64:6 tells us, "...all our righteousnesses are like filthy rags" in His sight. The very best that man has to offer is corrupted in God's eyes. Sin is detestable to God. Since He is also a just God, He made a way for dealing with sin.

On judgment day God will pour out His wrath against all unbelievers. In John 3:36 we are told, "He who believes in the Son has everlasting life; and he who does not believe the Son shall not see life, but the wrath of God abides on Him." Hell was created to be a place of punishment for those on whom God pours out His wrath. Romans 1:18 sheds light on this issue. In this Scripture we read, "...the wrath of God is revealed from heaven against all ungodliness and unrighteousness of men." Colossians 3:6 reminds us the "wrath of God is coming upon the sons of disobedience." Sin presents a problem for which a holy God must provide a solution. Since God deplores our sin, He must act against it.

Even though God is both loving and just, the human tendency is to focus only on His love, resulting in a rationalization of our behavior. Herein is man's problem. We have a 100% righteous and holy God who resides in heaven. Since heaven is a perfect place, how does mankind escape the wrath of God and make it to heaven? This is the ultimate question that every human being must contemplate. Since God cannot allow sin of any kind in heaven, how is sinful mankind able to spend eternity with the Lord?

God's Plan of Redemption

God has a plan to redeem us from our sins. God's plan of redemption was set in motion from the beginning of time and was completed when the Lord Jesus died on the cross and arose from the tomb after three days. The Bible gives many different terms to describe this plan. In John 3:3 Jesus said to Nicodemus, "unless one is born again, he cannot see the kingdom of God." Other passages state that we must be converted (Matthew 18:3, Acts 3:19). Another term often used is "being saved" (Ephesians 2:8, Acts 4:12, John 3:17). In Acts 11:26 and I Peter 4:16, we find the term "Christian" being used for those that had been redeemed by God. No matter which term you choose, the bottom line question is: How do I obtain this relationship with God?

John 14:6 reminds us that Jesus is the way to God. We must have a correct understanding of Jesus, if we are to find the Father. Through many Biblical references, it has been established that Jesus is God in the flesh. There is no further need to elaborate on that point. In I Corinthians 15:3-4 we read the rest of the Gospel: Jesus died for our sins, He was buried, and He rose again the third day.

The cross is a vital part of God's plan of redemption. The cross is a mystery to a non-believer. In fact, in I Corinthians 1:18 we read that "the message of the cross is foolishness to those that are perishing." Why Jesus had to die on a cross and its relevance is difficult for the unbeliever to grasp. In the Old Testament, God's plan for covering sins was offering animal sacrifices. In Leviticus 4:13-20 God tells the children of Israel to sacrifice a bull for their transgression. We also read there were different sacrifices required for various sins. The Lord commanded that the animals for sacrifices must be without blemish (Exodus 12:5, Leviticus 4:23, Numbers 6:14). Two things stand out here: 1) the animal sacrificed had to be perfect and 2) blood had to be shed. These were key requirements for gaining the forgiveness of God, as the people looked forward to Jesus' death on the cross, which would end all sacrifices (Hebrew 10:10-12). Jesus' death on the cross unleashed all the fury of God. Jesus took God's wrath over man's sin upon Himself and God accepted that sacrifice as payment for sin. Only Jesus could be the perfect, required, sacrifice. His death on the cross was the method God chose to redeem mankind.

The other element in I Corinthians 15:3-4 is the resurrection. Without the resurrection, Jesus would only have been a martyr who died for a good cause. The resurrection was God's final sign that the cross was His work. Since Jesus prophesied that He would rise the third day, His claims of being Messiah hinged on fulfilling that statement. Belief in His death on the cross and resurrection are paramount to being redeemed. Mankind's sin separated all people from a Holy God. Jesus bridged the gap through His death on the cross. However, that does not mean all sin is automatically redeemed. God has done His part in taking care of the sin problem, but man has a requirement, as well.

How to Be Saved

In the Gospels, Jesus commanded everyone to repent (Matthew 4:17, Mark 1:15, and Luke 13:3). In the book of Acts, the disciples preached the same message of repentance (Acts 2:38, 3:19, 17:30, and 26:20). In Christian circles, the term "repent" is probably one of the most misunderstood and misinterpreted doctrines of the Bible. We have all heard the expression "turn or burn," which implies a person must change behavior or go to hell. This phrase suggests that behavior dictates the eternal destiny of individuals. The truth is, only God's grace allows a person to stand without condemnation before a righteous and holy God. Behavior will never earn anyone a "ticket" to heaven. Entrance into heaven is only through the finished work of Jesus. Clearly, the Lord does care about personal behavior. He wants every person to glorify His Son after salvation. However, behavior does not get anyone into heaven.

The Greek word for repent is metaneo, which means to *change your mind*. All people need to change their minds about three things:[1]

1. We must change our mind about Jesus. The world teaches that Jesus was not deity and that He is only one of many ways to God. We must believe in the deity of Christ! He is not a way; He is THE WAY (John 14:6).

2. We must change our mind about sin. We must realize our sin is awful! We must come to grips with the fact that our sins have separated us from God (Romans 3:23). Man tries to downplay his sin by saying, "I am no worse than my neighbor," or "Everybody else is doing it." We need to view sin as God sees it. When we see our sin from God's perspective, our response should be to sorrow over our separation from Him and to repent (2 Corinthians 7:10). Until we deal with our sin, we are facing eternal separation

from God (Romans 6:23). Yes, we need to change our mind about sin.

3. We must change our mind about self. The secular humanists teach that man is continually getting better. They obviously are looking at intellectual accomplishments rather than morality. We must understand that we cannot come to God on our own merit. The Bible teaches that, "We have turned, every one, to his own way…" (Isaiah 53:6). No one will ever find favor with God on personal merit. We must realize that we are inherently sinful and cannot change on our own. The Good News is that because of God's plan of salvation, we have hope!

Biblical repentance is agreement with God about our sin and the realization that we need Him to change our lives. We don't have to stop sinning to be saved; rather, we need to be saved so that we can stop sinning! We recognize that only Jesus can change a life and give victory over sin (I Corinthians 15:57). Repentance is stating, "I'm sick and tired of being sick and tired and I know I need the Lord to change me." Man has the easy part (repentance); God has the hard part (changing us). As we learn to let Him work in our lives, change becomes easier and quicker.

Many have tried coming to God without Biblical repentance and have experienced the same result, which is failure. The scribes and Pharisees were the religious leaders during Jesus' time. They were self-seekers; they felt sufficient in themselves; and they rejected Jesus. They were in error, and Jesus denounced them as hypocrites (Matthew 23:25-33). No one will ever come to God without repentance. We must *change our minds!* We must let go of our self-life, and let God make us anew!

The Bible tells us that we must receive Christ (John 1:12). In Revelation 3:20 we read that Jesus is standing at the door of our individual lives and knocking. If anyone hears His voice and opens the door, He will come in.

It is not enough to know the truth; we must also act on it. We do not benefit from knowing what Jesus did for us if we do not invite Him into our lives. We receive Him by faith as our Savior. Through an act of our will, we ask Jesus to come into our lives. The Bible says God is a Spirit (John 4:24). That is where faith comes into play. We ask Jesus, whom we cannot see, to be our Savior. Only by God's grace does this take place (Ephesians 2:8-9). We will never earn or deserve salvation. The Revelation 3:20 passage refers to opening the door of my life to let Jesus come in. This door is unique in that it only has a doorknob on the inside. Jesus will not open the door because He gave each person a free will. Due to that provision, He cannot force a person to take any action. Each individual has 100% choice to open the door or leave it closed. By my own volition, the need for Jesus to change me and make me into a new creation is believed and received.

Salvation takes place in a mere moment of time. Although it may take years to reach this point, salvation occurs immediately upon receiving the Gospel into my heart. I must sincerely believe that Jesus is God in the flesh, that He died on the cross for my sins, and that He rose again the third day. I must also sincerely repent, acknowledge my personal sin, ask God's forgiveness, and realize the need for inner change. By faith, I must ask Jesus into my life as my personal Savior. I know I have received salvation, or am born again, after trusting Jesus Christ to take away my sins. That is how I *know* that I have entered into eternal life (I John 5:13, John 3:16, John 5:24, John 6:47, and John 10:27).

If you sincerely believe and want Jesus to come into your life, pray this prayer:

"Jesus, I believe you are God in the flesh. Thank you for dying on the cross for my sins and rising again the third day. I confess that I am a sinner, and I repent from all my sins. Please come into my life and be my Savior. Amen."

If you sincerely repented and invited Jesus into your life, you are now a new creation in Christ (2 Corinthians 5:17). Be assured that God has forgiven all your sins (Psalm 103:12, Romans 3:24) and guarantees you eternal life. In addition, from now on, Jesus is with you to help you work out the issues of life (Philippians 4:13).

Closing

I remember a conversation with a young adult several years ago. This individual did not believe in God and questioned what the Bible says. He asked me, "What happens if you are wrong and there is no God?" I replied, "I will have lived a good moral life built on helping others, and I will have been a positive influence in the world for good." Then I asked him, "What happens if you are wrong?" After a long discussion, we finally agreed on two things: 1) If he is wrong, his life on earth will have been an entire waste, completely missing the point of why he was created and 2) he will be in hell for all of eternity. I ask you: Which one of us do you think has the most to lose?

Notes

1. C.I. Scofield, *The New Schofield Study Bible*, New King James Version, Footnote #4 on Acts 17:30, (Nashville: Thomas Nelson Publishers, 1989) 1343.

Biography

Don Anderson entered full-time correctional ministry in 1984, focusing on evangelism and discipleship in jails, prisons, and juvenile halls in California and Texas. For the past seventeen years he has been on staff with Pacific Youth Correctional Ministries. Since 1992 Don has served as regional director for the Dallas-Fort Worth area. As an ordained minister and licensed corrections chaplain, Don comes into frequent contact with people from many religious backgrounds. Many of these individuals are uncertain or in error about the main difference between Christianity and other beliefs. Study and teaching to provide clarity on this topic developed into FOR HEAVEN'S SAKE: WHO IS JESUS?

For More Information See Our Website:
sowhoisJesus.com

Don Anderson
P.O. Box 120634
Arlington, Texas 76012